Iain Spragg
& Adrian Clarke

LEWIS
HAMILTON

Bath · New York · Singapore · Hong Kong · Cologne · Delhi · Melbourne

Contents

GO GO The

boy racer

Formula One has found itself a new phenomenon in the shape of McLaren Mercedes driver Lewis Hamilton. Little known outside Grand Prix until early 2007, the rookie driver quite simply stunned the sporting world with a succession of brilliant performances, tearing up the record books in the process. But the road to fame was far from short, beginning way back in 1993 when an eager eight-year-old began competing in go-kart races at his local Hertfordshire track. It quickly became apparent that the youngster was a natural.

Making of a legend

Born in Stevenage, Hertfordshire, on 7 January 1985, Lewis Hamilton had an instant attraction to cars from a very young age. So much so in fact that his father Anthony and stepmother Linda spent three quarters of their monthly salary on a £1,000 go-kart for his Christmas present at the age of just six. Within two years the car-mad youngster was ready to take to the track and young Lewis soon began competing in local karting events. Within two years Hamilton had swept all before him in his age bracket, winning the prestigious McLaren Champions of the Future series. Racing was an expensive business, however, and with a modest income his parents struggled to support their son's interest. But with extreme faith in Lewis, proud dad Anthony worked three different jobs to make sure his boy had the best possible opportunity to develop his natural talent.

By the age of 10, Hamilton was already a highly-rated karting driver, winning several major competitions at junior level. The naturally gifted youngster (below) was driven to succeed and was already dreaming of a career in Formula One when he left school.

Hamilton's progress as an emerging talent hadn't gone unnoticed by the Formula One hierarchy and it wasn't long before the 10-year-old was introduced to McLaren boss Ron Dennis. The youngster is reported to have cheekily said on that first meeting: "I'm going to race for you one day. I'm going to race for McLaren." The team supremo kept a close eye on his progress, seeing him win the Super One British Championship (1995 and 1997), the Sky TV Kart Masters Championship (1996) and the Champions of the Future series (1996 and 1997). Hamilton's reputation within the racing fraternity was growing fast and it was clear that the teenager possessed a special talent behind the wheel that set him apart from his peers. Lewis Hamilton was being earmarked for bigger and better things. His lifelong dream of becoming a professional racing driver was looking like it might really become a reality.

Just days before the 2007 British Grand Prix at Silverstone, Lewis Hamilton returned to the Daytona go-karting circuit in Milton Keynes, the scene of some of his greatest triumphs as a junior karting champion. On hand to give coaching tips to a select group of children competing at the British Racing Drivers 'Stars of Tomorrow' event, it was obvious that Hamilton has nothing but fond memories of his karting days. "This is where I learnt my racing craft," he told the awe-struck youngsters. "The manoeuvres you see me use in F1, I wouldn't have had without karting."

It seemed that Hamilton's rapid rise to stardom in 2007 had already had a major impact on the number of kids looking to take part in motor sport at a young age. The Daytona track doubled the number of children racing there in 12 months and much of that was put down to the 'Lewis Hamilton effect'. As well as passing on advice to the future stars of Formula One (above right), the Grand Prix star also presented the winner's trophy to 11-year-old Suffolk driver Alex Albon (above left), winner of the day's event.

A star in waiting 1998

JOINING A WINNING TEAM

Sensing that they might have a future world champion on their hands as early as 1998, Team McLaren signed Lewis Hamilton up to their driver development support programme. The financial burden previously carried by his family was now taken up by the team, who included an option in his contract stating that he had a future drive in their F1 car. This made 13-year-old Hamilton the youngest ever driver to secure a Formula One contract. The teenager's progress grew apace – despite the security guaranteed him by the contract – as the Hertfordshire-born prodigy continued to lift a series of major international titles. The 1999 season saw Hamilton become Intercontinental A champion and Junior ICA Vice European champion. A maximum points total gave him the Formula A European Championship the following year, while shortly after he was named as karting's world number one.

McLaren Mercedes announce that 21-year-old GP2 champion Lewis Hamilton will join their Formula One team for the 2007 season (left). The highly-rated driver immediately impressed the team management with some excellent displays in testing for the new season. (right)

At 16, McLaren decided to hand their most prized asset a seat in a racing car for the first time and it didn't take long for the youngster to adapt to life after karting, finishing a creditable fifth in the British Formula Renault series. Within two years he'd captured the title and in 2004 he was promoted to the F3 Euroseries. After two seasons he was champion again, at the tender age of 20.

(top left) Hamilton celebrates his seat in the 2007 McLaren Mercedes car with team boss Ron Dennis. (above and right) Mika Häkkinen and David Coulthard were the two McLaren drivers when Hamilton joined the team in 1998.

Hamilton gives fans the thumbs-up after lifting the
GP2 series at the first attempt in 2006 for the ART
team. Next stop Formula One!

GP2 Series
2005

After dominating Formula Three in 2005, Hamilton won a seat on the highly-rated ART Grand Prix GP2 team. It was to prove a sensational season for the rising star as he won the championship with ease at the first attempt. With five wins to his name, including a double at Silverstone before the 2006 British Grand Prix, and a triumph on the streets of Monte Carlo, it was apparent that McLaren's leading prospect's development had come as far as it could go before they unleashed him on Formula One. At 21, it was seen as a gamble to hand one of their prized seats to an inexperienced rookie, but boss Ron Dennis had seen enough to know that it was a gamble he was prepared to take.

(top) The 21-year-old rushes straight towards father Anthony after clinching the GP2 title at Monza. (middle) Hamilton poses with the trophy after his second place at Monza secured him the GP2 World Championship. (bottom) The GP2 champion is a dab hand with the champagne on the podium. (main left) Young Lewis Hamilton is already in the sights of Formula One star Felipe Massa.

A F1 rookie's

Despite his reputation for only recruiting proven drivers, McLaren-Mercedes chief Ron Dennis had no doubt that his 22-year-old protégé Lewis Hamilton was ready to make the giant leap into Formula One for the 2007 season. Nine years of careful nurturing had transformed the karting wonder kid into the hottest property outside Grand Prix and Dennis was refusing to hold his starlet back any longer. It was time to show the world his most prized young asset. Surprisingly, Hamilton's 2006 GP2 championship-winning campaign had failed to convince everybody that he was

year 2007

the 'real deal'. In fact, as the Stevenage-born youngster prepared for his debut Grand Prix in Melbourne, the critics were queuing up to pronounce that champion Fernando Alonso's new team-mate didn't have the necessary strength of character to handle the pressure that came with such a coveted seat at the highest level. Unperturbed, there were no obvious signs of nerves from Hamilton – only quietly-assured confidence. But how would the untested rookie fare when the heat was really on? We were about to find out....

Canadian Grand Prix
Montreal 10 June 2007

Just when Lewis Hamilton thought his debut season couldn't get any better, it did with a magnificently crafted victory at the Canadian Grand Prix in Montreal. After claiming the first pole position of his short career at the Gilles Villeneuve circuit, the rookie sensation led from start to finish and in doing so became the first black driver to win a Formula One Grand Prix. Robert Kubica's horrific crash and several other incidents during the race led to the safety car being employed on four occasions, but Hamilton refused to let it affect his concentration and produced a faultless drive. Team-mate Fernando Alonso had a nightmare race finishing seventh and bitterly described Hamilton's win as "very lucky" afterwards although most experts were full of praise for the Englishman.

Lewis gives the victory sign (top), having successfully completed the 70 laps starting and finishing in first position (above and opposite).

#2 Lewis Hamilton

Hamilton's popularity began to reach fever pitch in Canada with Union Jack flags seen all around the Montreal circuit. His humble and well-mannered personality off the track has unquestionably won him hordes of new fans both sides of the Atlantic, but there was no question that his brave racing style marked him out as a future world champion. Hamilton's parade car may have been number two but the rookie already had his eye on becoming Grand Prix's undisputed number one.

Pole position holder Hamilton waves to his legion of adoring fans in Montreal on the traditional pre-race drivers' parade around the Gilles Villeneuve circuit.

The young Englishman punches his fist with delight shortly after taking the chequered flag for the first time in his career – incredibly in only his sixth Formula One Grand Prix.

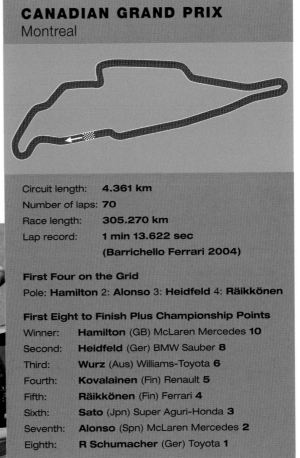

CANADIAN GRAND PRIX
Montreal

Circuit length:	4.361 km
Number of laps:	70
Race length:	305.270 km
Lap record:	1 min 13.622 sec
	(Barrichello Ferrari 2004)

First Four on the Grid
Pole: **Hamilton** 2: **Alonso** 3: **Heidfeld** 4: **Räikkönen**

First Eight to Finish Plus Championship Points

Winner:	**Hamilton** (GB) McLaren Mercedes **10**
Second:	**Heidfeld** (Ger) BMW Sauber **8**
Third:	**Wurz** (Aus) Williams-Toyota **6**
Fourth:	**Kovalainen** (Fin) Renault **5**
Fifth:	**Räikkönen** (Fin) Ferrari **4**
Sixth:	**Sato** (Jpn) Super Aguri-Honda **3**
Seventh:	**Alonso** (Spn) McLaren Mercedes **2**
Eighth:	**R Schumacher** (Ger) Toyota **1**

US Grand Prix
Indianapolis 17 June 2007

The incredible fairytale start to life in Formula One for Lewis Hamilton continued apace at the famous Indianapolis Motor Speedway circuit as the McLaren Mercedes star registered a second successive pole position and second race victory in a row. Pressed fiercely by team-mate Alonso throughout the 73-lap race, the British star kept his nerve superbly to open up a ten point lead at the top of the drivers' championship table.

US GRAND PRIX
Indianapolis

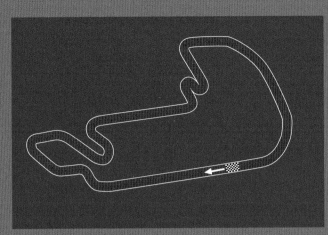

Circuit length: **4.192 km**
Number of laps: **73**
Race length: **306.016 km**
Lap record: **1 min 10.399 sec**
                   (Barrichello Ferrari 2004)

First Four on the Grid
Pole: **Hamilton** 2: **Alonso** 3: **Massa** 4: **Räikkönen**

First Eight to Finish Plus Championship Points
Winner: **Hamilton** (GB) McLaren Mercedes **10**
Second: **Alonso** (Spn) McLaren Mercedes **8**
Third: **Massa** (Bra) Ferrari **6**
Fourth: **Räikkönen** (Fin) Ferrari **5**
Fifth: **Kovalainen** (Fin) Renault **4**
Sixth: **Trulli** (Ita) Toyota **3**
Seventh: **Webber** (Aus) Red Bull-Renault **2**
Eighth: **Vettel** (Ger) BMW Sauber **1**

UNITED STATES GRAND PRIX

For the second successive race Hamilton is first to take the chequered flag (main) in front of the packed grandstand. The Union Jack flag is raised as the youngster sings along to the national anthem on the podium at Indianapolis. (above)

Budapest

Controversy reigned at the Hungaroring after Fernando Alonso was sensationally demoted from pole position to sixth on the grid for deliberately impeding team-mate Hamilton during final qualification. Lewis gained sweet revenge on the Spaniard. The victory extended Hamilton's lead to seven points in the drivers' standings and his title prospects were looking good.

HUNGARIAN GRAND PRIX
Budapest

Circuit length: **4.381 km**

Number of laps: **70**

Race length: **306.663 km**

Lap record: **1 min 19.1071 sec**

                    (M Schumacher Ferrari 2004)

First Four on the Grid

Pole: **Alonso** 2: **Hamilton** 3: **Heidfeld** 4: **Räikkönen**

First Eight to Finish Plus Championships Points

Winner:	**Hamilton** (GB) McLaren Mercedes	**10**
Second:	**Räikkönen** (Fin) Ferrari	**8**
Third:	**Heidfeld** (Ger) BMW Sauber	**6**
Fourth:	**Alonso** (Spn) McLaren Mercedes	**5**
Fifth:	**Kubica** (Pol) BMW Sauber	**4**
Sixth:	**R Schumacher** (Ger) Toyota	**3**
Seventh:	**Rosberg** (Ger) Williams-Toyota	**2**
Eighth:	**Kovalainen** (Fin) Renault	**1**

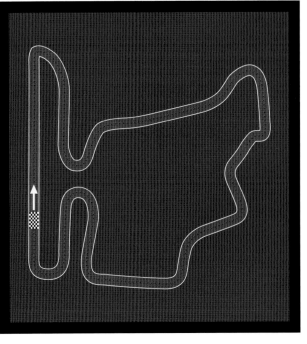

A fiercely competitive effort from Ferrari's Kimi Räikkönen pushed Hamilton all the way in Budapest with just half a second separating the duo for several laps of the contest. (left)

Following the unsavoury behaviour of team-mate Alonso in qualifying, Hamilton was pumped up like never before after claiming the win in Hungary – and he wasn't afraid to show it as he was greeted by his McLaren team in the pits. (below left)

After racking up 80 points in the drivers' championship and extending his lead to seven points in the process, it was little wonder that Hamilton felt like kissing the ornate trophy awarded to him on the podium. (below right)

Japanese Grand Prix
Shizuoka 30 September 2007

After a 30-year absence, the Fuji Speedway made a welcome return to the Formula One calendar with a weekend that proved to be the sternest of tests for all the drivers as wet weather dominated proceedings in Japan. A tricky qualifying session on a slippery track created thrills and spills aplenty but it was the McLaren duo of Lewis Hamilton and Fernando Alonso who were sat on the front row for the start of the big race, ahead of the menacing Ferrari pair of Massa and Räikkönen .

The heavens opened on race day with persistent rain creating treacherous conditions. With visibility and grip in short supply, the safety car had to lead the field around the track for the opening 19 laps but once free to race, the drivers produced a dramatic spectacle and the individual performance of the season – in the shape of Hamilton's stunning drive.

It was a performance which showcased every ounce of skill and talent the 22-year-old had at his disposal and proved beyond doubt that he had what it took to be a world champion.

Starting on pole alongside team-mate Alonso, a brave surge from lap 19 onwards saw Hamilton quickly open up a lead over his competitors as heavy spray made driving conditions a nightmare for everyone behind him. (left)

An unlucky spin created by some erratic driving from BMW Sauber's Robert Kubica left Hamilton fans with their hearts in their mouths but the unflappable rookie held his nerve, keeping his McLaren on the track for the remainder of the race despite late pressure from Heikki Kovalainen and Kimi Räikkönen . (right)

JAPANESE GRAND PRIX
Shizuoka

Circuit length:	**4.563 km**
Number of laps:	**67**
Race length:	**305.721 km**
Lap record:	**1 min 28.193 sec**
	(L Hamilton McLaren Mercedes 2007)

First Four on the Grid
Pole: **Hamilton** 2: **Alonso** 3: **Räikkönen** 4: **Massa**

First Eight to Finish Plus Championship Points

Winner:	**Hamilton** (GB) McLaren Mercedes	**10**
Second:	**Kovalainen** (Fin) Renault	**8**
Third:	**Räikkönen** (Fin) Ferrari	**6**
Fourth:	**Coulthard** (GB) Red Bull-Renault	**5**
Fifth:	**Fisichella** (Ita) Renault	**4**
Sixth:	**Massa** (Bra) Ferrari	**3**
Seventh:	**Kubica** (Pol) BMW Sauber	**2**
Eighth:	**Sutil** (Ger) Spyker-Ferrari	**1**

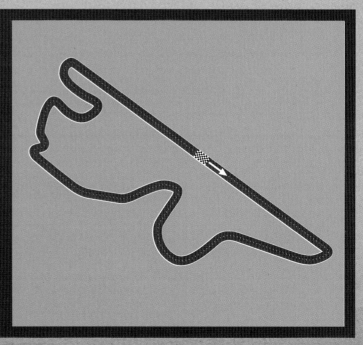

Appalling conditions and a mid-race spin could not shake the young Englishman's resolve as Hamilton coolly produced the drive of his life to take the chequered flag in front of a rain-sodden crowd in Shizuoka. (below) It was a victory that left the rookie 17 points clear in the drivers' championship.

Second-placed Heikki Kovalainen looks rightly satisfied as he is pictured with a smiling victor on the podium at the conclusion of what turned out to be a thrilling 15th race of the season. (near right)

With his fourth Formula One win under his belt and a clear margin over his title rivals in the drivers' championship, it was little wonder Hamilton's celebrations in Shizuoka were exuberant. (far right)

With just two races remaining, the seemingly unflappable rookie was now leading the drivers' table by an astonishing 17 points. Only a major catastrophe in both China and Brazil could prevent Hamilton from making history by becoming the first black driver to win the Championship.

Incredibly, that disastrous scenario happened. A spin in China followed by a seventh place finish in Brazil, coupled with two brilliant Kimi Räikkönen victories, left Hamilton shaking his head in disbelief.

In his first F1 season he had been beaten to the title by a single point in his debut season.

A F1 winner's

A disappointed but proud Lewis Hamilton found it difficult to relax after his thrilling, yet ultimately frustrating debut season in Formula One. For the English flying machine, F1's 147-day break was agony as he waited desperately for the chance to make amends for the calamities in China and Brazil that had cost him the title.

Hamilton came back a more confident figure, however. Months of winter testing in McLaren's revamped car had gone well and alongside him in the garage was a new, more amiable team-mate in the form of Heikki Kovalainen. As

year 2008

undisputed number one at McLaren, the frustrations that had soured his relationship with Fernando Alonso in 2007 were now put to one side.

On the eve of the 2008 season, Hamilton claimed he was 'better prepared, more relaxed and hungrier' than he had been a year before. And as he prepared for the opening Grand Prix of the year in Melbourne, there was an air of self-assurance about Hamilton that gave the distinct impression that he was ready to hit the ground running....

Australian Grand Prix
Melbourne 16 March 2008

If Lewis Hamilton was attempting to prove a point to the world on his return to the track in 2008, he

certainly succeeded in doing so at Albert Park. In his gleaming new McLaren Mercedes car, the 23-

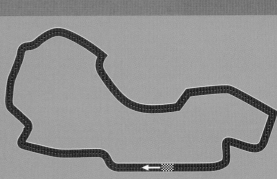

AUSTRALIAN GRAND PRIX
Melbourne

Circuit length: **5.303 km**
Number of laps: **58**
Race length: **307.574 km**
Lap record: **1 min 24.125 sec**
(M Schumacher Ferrari 2004)

First Four on the Grid
Pole: **Hamilton** 2: **Kubica** 3: **Kovalainen** 4: **Massa**

First Eight to Finish Plus Championship Points

Winner:	**Hamilton** (GB) McLaren Mercedes **10**	
Second:	**Heidfeld** (Ger) BMW Sauber **8**	
Third:	**Rosberg** (Ger) Williams-Toyota **6**	
Fourth:	**Alonso** (Spn) Renault **5**	
Fifth:	**Kovalainen** (Fin) McLaren Mercedes **4**	
Sixth:	**Nakajima** (Jap) Williams-Toyota **3**	
Seventh:	**Bourdais** (Fre) STR-Ferrari **2**	
Eighth:	**Räikkönen** (Fin) Ferrari **1**	

year-old simply cruised through qualification, comfortably grabbing pole position ahead of surprise

package Robert Kubica in the BMW Sauber and Heikki Kovalainen. With an air temperature of 37

degrees and a burning sun shining brightly in the blue Melbourne sky, everyone was feeling the heat

as they lined up on the grid. However, as the lights went out there was one driver who appeared to

be far cooler than the rest as they raced towards the opening bend...and that was Hamilton.

From lap one to 58, Lewis Hamilton drove a near flawless race to obliterate the field. All the dramas of a crazy race occurred behind the McLaren as just seven cars made it to the finish line but for Hamilton it was plain sailing as both his car and driving technique survived the challenges of the testing street circuit. Hamilton's winning margin of five seconds over Nick Heidfeld belied the comfort of this victory.

Hamilton salutes his fans after taking the chequered flag at Albert Park, comprehensively winning the Australian Grand Prix in the much-anticipated opening race of the 2008 season. (left)

It was a near-perfect day for the McLaren Mercedes team as Hamilton and Kovalainen, who finished third, enjoyed their champagne moment on the winners' podium in front of a huge and excited Melbourne crowd. (below)

There was no doubt who was the biggest attraction in town all weekend as supporters clamoured to get a glimpse of their new hero – with a few lucky fans managing to grab an autograph from F1's most exciting and popular driver. (bottom)

Monaco Grand Prix 25 May 2008

Monte Carlo

Hamilton's success in Australia was singular in an otherwise indifferent start to the season, so the Englishman arrived in Monte Carlo for race six, trailing Kimi Räikkönen and level on points with Felipe Massa. The star had always dreamed of winning the Monaco Grand Prix and after an impressive second-place finish in 2007, he was understandably eager to go one better. Unfortunately, the Brazilian Massa produced a stunning lap in the final qualifying session to take pole.

An unexpected rain storm gave Hamilton renewed hope that he could win from third on the grid. Famed for his skill in wet conditions, this played right into his hands and by the time the cars reached turn one he was already breathing down Massa's neck in second place. Apparent disaster then struck six laps later with Hamilton puncturing a rear tyre after colliding with a barrier near the swimming pool – but his unscheduled pit stop was to be the defining moment of the race.

MONACO GRAND PRIX
Monte Carlo

Circuit length:	**3.340 km**
Number of laps:	**78**
Race length:	**260.520 km**
Lap record:	**1 min 14.439 sec**
	(M Schumacher Ferrari 2004)

First Four on the Grid
Pole: **Massa** 2: **Räikkönen** 3: **Hamilton** 4: **Kovalainen**

First Eight to Finish Plus Championship Points

Winner:	**Hamilton** (GB) McLaren Mercedes **10**
Second:	**Kubica** (Pol) BMW Sauber **8**
Third:	**Massa** (Bra) Ferrari **6**
Fourth:	**Webber** (Aus) Red Bull-Renault **5**
Fifth:	**Vettel** (Ger) STR-Ferrari **4**
Sixth:	**Barrichello** (Bra) Honda **3**
Seventh:	**Nakajima** (Jap) Williams-Toyota **2**
Eighth:	**Kovalainen** (Fin) McLaren Mercedes **1**

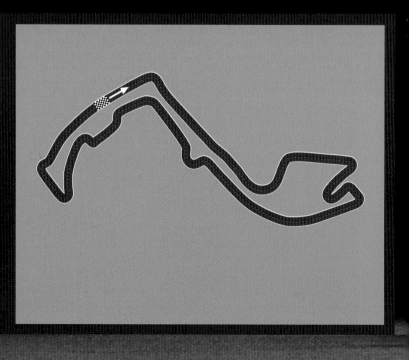

World champion Kimi Räikkönen rejoins the race behind third-placed Lewis Hamilton on lap 13 after being handed a drive-through penalty by officials for fitting his tyres too close to the start of the Grand Prix. It was to be the first of several setbacks throughout the afternoon for the frustrated Finn. (right)

Hamilton's puncture on lap six allowed McLaren to pour enough extra fuel into the car to finish the race. The drying track also aided Lewis. On lap 76, with the race exceeding its two-hour limit, an ecstatic Hamilton crossed the finishing line in first position. It was a lifelong dream fulfilled.

The McLaren pit crew celebrate wildly as their main title contender regains the championship lead. (above)

Pussycat Dolls singer Nicole Scherzinger, Hamilton's girlfriend, and rap star P Diddy watch nervously. (above right)

A thrilled Hamilton jumps for joy as he exits the cockpit after winning in Monte Carlo. (right)

Silverstone 6 July 2008

Britain's racing superstar arrived at his home Grand Prix under intense pressure, having finished the previous two races without scoring any point. The knives were out for him in the press but despite his lack of form, Hamilton remained convinced he would land a famous victory in front of his adoring fans. Qualification didn't go according to plan for the McLaren star however, as team-mate Heikki Kovalainen earned a shock pole with a frustrated Hamilton having to settle for a place on the second row on the grid. With

90,000 British fans pouring through the Silverstone gates, the home favourite was given a timely boost as the dark clouds overhead created a steady stream of rain that made conditions treacherous. Hamilton simply flew off the grid with a blistering start that saw him gain two places before the first corner. Crucially, the only man now ahead of him was team-mate Kovalainen.

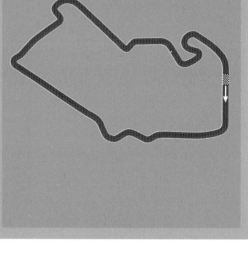

BRITISH GRAND PRIX
Silverstone

Circuit length:	**5.141 km**
Number of laps:	**60**
Race length:	**308.355 km**
Lap record:	**1 min 18.739 sec**
	(M Schumacher Ferrari 2004)

First Four on the Grid
Pole: **Kovalainen** 2: **Webber** 3: **Räikkönen** 4: **Hamilton**

First Eight to Finish Plus Championship Points

Winner:	**Hamilton** (GB) McLaren Mercedes	**10**
Second:	**Heidfeld** (Ger) BMW Sauber	**8**
Third:	**Barrichello** (Bra) Honda	**6**
Fourth:	**Räikkönen** (Fin) Ferrari	**5**
Fifth:	**Kovalainen** (Fin) McLaren Mercedes	**4**
Sixth:	**Alonso** (Spn) Renault	**3**
Seventh:	**Trulli** (Ita) Toyota	**2**
Eighth:	**Nakajima** (Jap) Williams-Toyota	**1**

Hamilton crossed the line to become the first Briton since David Coulthard to win at Silverstone. (above)

Nick Heidfeld and Rubens Barrichello join Hamilton on the podium as the 23-year-old celebrates. (right)

A proud moment for the Stevenage-born driver as he holds aloft the beautiful trophy. (inset)

After passing Kovalainen on lap five, Hamilton opened up a healthy advantage on the chasing pack but was soon put under pressure from a fierce Räikkönen charge. With the rain abating both drivers pitted on lap 21 but it was McLaren's decision to fit their man with wet weather tyres that proved decisive as just minutes later the skies opened with another deluge of rain. It was the slice of luck Hamilton had been waiting for.

From then on it was an absolute procession as Hamilton produced a near perfect drive. As the drivers in his slip stream struggled to stay on the track, his superlative talent was there for all to see.

German Grand Prix
Hockenheim 20 July 2008

Boosted by his superb performance at Silverstone, Hamilton was eager to record back-to-back victories with a win at Hockenheim – and during qualification he once again showed his burning desire to succeed. Trailing Felipe Massa with just one flying lap remaining, Lewis dug deep to pull off a sensational drive, narrowly beating his Ferrari rival to pole by just two tenths of a second. With thousands of German Mercedes fans cheering him from the stands, the weight of support was once again with Hamilton.

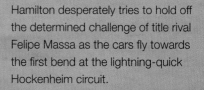

Hamilton desperately tries to hold off the determined challenge of title rival Felipe Massa as the cars fly towards the first bend at the lightning-quick Hockenheim circuit.

GERMAN GRAND PRIX
Hockenheim

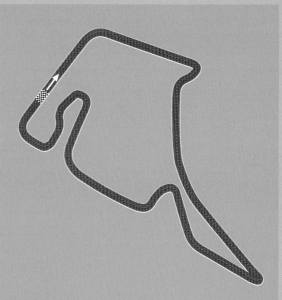

Circuit length: **4.574 km**

Number of laps: **67**

Race length: **306.458 km**

Lap record: **1 min 13.780 sec**

(K Räikkönen McLaren 2004)

First Four on the Grid

Pole: **Hamilton** 2: **Massa** 3: **Kovalainen** 4: **Trulli**

First Eight to Finish Plus Championship Points

Winner:	**Hamilton** (GB) McLaren Mercedes	**10**
Second:	**Piquet** (Bra) Renault	**8**
Third:	**Massa** (Bra) Ferrari	**6**
Fourth:	**Heidfeld** (Ger) BMW Sauber	**5**
Fifth:	**Kovalainen** (Fin) McLaren Mercedes	**4**
Sixth:	**Räikkönen** (Fin) Ferrari	**3**
Seventh:	**Kubica** (Pol) BMW Sauber	**2**
Eighth:	**Vettel** (Ger) STR-Ferrari	**1**

A member of the McLaren Mercedes crew nervously awaits the arrival of Hamilton in the pit lane as the Briton is forced to change tyres at the most inopportune moment possible. It was a pit stop that cost him five places. (above)

Hamilton's half-brother Nicholas greets his hero in the garage with a beaming smile and embrace after watching the McLaren star produce a breathtaking comeback at Hockenheim to win the German Grand Prix. (main)

Hamilton drops his winner's magnum of champagne down to a posse of celebrating McLaren Mercedes team-mates after pulling off an incredible late fight back to win his fourth race of the season. (top right)

Holding the winner's trophy aloft, a smiling Hamilton knew that his four point lead over Felipe Massa in the drivers' championship could turn out to be crucial as they entered the final few weeks of the campaign. (bottom right)

Hamilton's start to the German Grand Prix was nothing short of sensational as he pulled away from the field. However, a major crash involving Timo Glock unluckily disrupted the Briton's virtuoso display and after the deployment of the safety car, the McLaren Mercedes star found himself in fifth place with just 16 laps remaining.

Refusing to give up on the win, Hamilton cut through the field, bravely passing Massa to take second place and eventually cruising past Nelson Piquet Jnr on lap 60 of 67. McLaren's first win at the track for ten long years was finally in the bag.

Chinese Grand Prix
Shanghai 19 October 2008

Hamilton arrived in Shanghai on the back of a poor 12th place performance in Japan but his pain was eased by the knowledge that the only man likely to prevent him from realising his dream of becoming 2008 world champion was Felipe Massa. It was now a two-horse race and one of them was certain to become F1 king for the very first time.

Qualification was all-important and the McLaren number one didn't disappoint when the pressure was on, clocking a brilliant 1:36.303 to land yet another pole position, two places ahead of Massa. No other pole in his superb 34-race career to date could have been more crucial.

CHINESE GRAND PRIX
Shanghai

Circuit length: **5.451 km**
Number of laps: **56**
Race length: **305.066 km**
Lap record: **1 min 32.238 sec**
                    (M Schumacher Ferrari 2004)

First Four on the Grid
Pole: **Hamilton** 2: **Räikkönen** 3: **Massa** 4: **Alonso**

First Eight to Finish Plus Championship Points
Winner: **Hamilton** (GB) McLaren Mercedes **10**
Second: **Massa** (Bra) Ferrari **8**
Third: **Räikkönen** (Fin) Ferrari **6**
Fourth: **Alonso** (Spn) Renault **5**
Fifth: **Heidfeld** (Ger) BMW Sauber **4**
Sixth: **Kubica** (Pol) BMW Sauber **3**
Seventh: **Glock** (Ger) Toyota **2**
Eighth: **Piquet** (Bra) Renault **1**

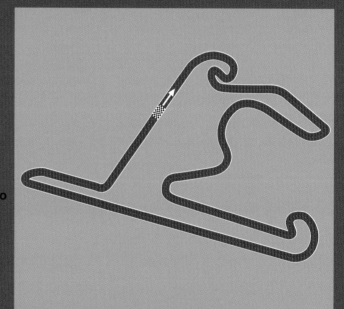

Having safely negotiated the nerve-jangling start, Hamilton was in imperious form around the Shanghai International Circuit and powered away from the rest of the field with cool precision. Everything went perfectly to plan for Hamilton who produced a faultless drive. His ninth career victory gave the 23-year-old star a much-needed seven point cushion ahead of the season finale. A fifth place finish in Brazil would now guarantee him the title.

By lap 14 Hamilton had opened up a staggering 12.2 second lead over Kimi Räikkönen , who later allowed team-mate Massa to pass him – handing the Brazilian two valuable extra points. (left)

Hamilton takes the most-valuable chequered flag of his career in Shanghai in front of an incredible 150,000 fans packed into the grandstands. (main)

The British superstar kisses yet another winner's trophy on the podium in China – but his thoughts were already on the season's climax in Brazil. (above)

Brazilian Grand Prix
São Paulo 2 November 2008

For the second successive season Britain's great F1 hope touched down on Brazilian soil leading the drivers' championship table with just one race remaining. With the world's eyes upon him, Hamilton was keen to stress that his error-strewn seventh place finish in São Paulo twelve months earlier wasn't an issue, but memories of his last visit to Interlagos must have been on his mind.

Needing to finish fifth to become champion, final qualifying didn't go according to plan for Hamilton who could only manage fourth place on the grid. Crucially his championship rival Massa was on pole with 100,000 F1 fans fervently behind him.

Holding aloft the Union Jack, a proud Lewis Hamilton reminds everyone he is the new number one after triumphantly becoming the youngest ever Formula One world champion. (right)

A nervous start from Hamilton in changeable weather conditions saw him initially drop back to sixth position but by the halfway stage he'd safely climbed back into the all-important fifth place. With Massa cruising in front, Hamilton's destiny remained in his own hands.

Suddenly, with eight laps left, a rain shower changed everything and he was overtaken by Sebastian Vettel and relegated to sixth. His only hope was to catch Toyota's Timo Glock and making up an astonishing 18 seconds on the final lap, Hamilton managed to pass the beleaguered Glock on the final bend. The 23-year-old Hamilton was world champion.

BRAZILIAN GRAND PRIX
São Paulo

Circuit length: **4.309 km**
Number of laps: **71**
Race length: **305.909 km**
Lap record: **1 min 11.473 sec**
(JP Montoya Williams-BMW 2004)

First Four on the Grid
Pole: **Massa** 2: **Trulli** 3: **Räikkönen** 4: **Hamilton**

First Eight to Finish Plus Championship Points
Winner:	**Massa** (Bra) Ferrari	**10**
Second:	**Alonso** (Spn) Renault	**8**
Third:	**Räikkönen** (Fin) Ferrari	**6**
Fourth:	**Vettel** (Ger) STR-Ferrari	**5**
Fifth:	**Hamilton** (GB) McLaren Mercedes	**4**
Sixth:	**Glock** (Ger) Toyota	**3**
Seventh:	**Kovalainen** (Fin) McLaren Mercedes	**2**
Eighth:	**Trulli** (Ita) Toyota	**1**

The world's media clamoured to get an immediate reaction from an exhausted Hamilton after his last-lap brilliance clinched the most dramatic world championship in F1 history – but McLaren's star man was intent on greeting his team-mates first. (left)

Britain's newest sporting hero poses for a celebratory team photo with the McLaren team with an arm around his proud and excited half-brother Nicholas, who suffers from cerebral palsy. (below)

Hamilton's girlfriend Nicole Scherzinger thinks her man is the number one driver in the world – and after watching his amazing win in São Paulo, who would disagree? (right)

61

At the age of just 23, Hamilton has rewritten the record books and made an indelible mark on British sporting history. After two magic seasons, the early signs suggest that he could even surpass Ayrton Senna's great achievements.

The Lewis Hamilton story is only just beginning....

Hamilton headed straight to team headquarters on his return to England where he thanked 1,000 delighted employees for their help in achieving his dream, passionately pledging his future to McLaren. Here he is pictured with the staff and brother Nicholas. (centre)

A much-deserved ticker tape reception was given to Hamilton as he met colleagues at McLaren's HQ in Woking, Surrey. The smiling driver is pictured here with just some of the silverware he collected in 2008. (right)

Proud McLaren chief Ron Dennis joins in the applause for his young protégé. The highly-experienced technical director is like a father figure to the star, having spotted his talent at the age of just 13. (above)

Picture Credits

All images in this book are courtesy of Getty Images including the following which have additional attributions:

11: Toshifumi Kitamura/ Agence France Presse; 16: Lars Baron/ Bongarts; 26: Gabriel Bouys/ Agence France Presse; 30: Bertrand Guay/ Agence France Presse; 32: Toru Yamanaka/ Agence France Presse; 33: Toru Yamanaka/ Agence France Presse; 35tl: Yoshikazu Tsuno/ Agence France Presse; 35tr: Toshifumi Kitamura/ Agence France Presse; 36-37: Vladimir Rys/Bongarts; 40: William West/ Agence France Presse; 41tr: William West/ Agence France Presse; 44: Pascal Guyot/ Agence France Presse; 45tr: Pascal Guyot/ Agence France Presse; 45br: Bertrand Guay/ Agence France Presse; 48: Bertrand Guay/ Agence France Presse; 49t: Shaun Curry/ Agence France Presse; 49br: Vladimir Rys/ Bongarts; 50-51: Bertrand Guay/ Agence France Presse; 55tr: Mark Ralston/ Agence France Presse; 56tl: Mark Ralston/ Agence France Presse; 56-57m: Goh Chai Hin/ Agence France Presse; 59tr: Antonio Scorza/ Agence France Presse

First edition published in 2007.

Parragon Books Ltd
Queen Street House
4 Queen Street
Bath BA1 1HE

Copyright © Endeavour London Ltd. 2009
This edition published by Parragon Books Ltd 2009

ISBN 978-1-4075-6834-8

ENDEAVOUR LONDON LTD
info@endeavourlondon.com

Created by Endeavour London Ltd.

Text: Iain Spragg and Adrian Clarke
Picture Research: Ben Bonarius, Mark Wieland, Franziska Payer Crockett
Art Direction: Paul Welti
Design Realisation: Keith Holmes
Artworks: Keith Holmes
Project Coordinator: Liz Ihre

Printed in Poland